Edited and typeset
Jessica C. Webb
Gifted Publishing Inc.
59 Main St., Suite 321
West Orange, New Jersey 07052

Self-published by Arthur DeBose

Dedication Page

First and foremost, I would like to give honor to God who through only his grace and mercy has allowed me to reach this point in my life and to complete this first book. Secondly, I would like to thank my Mom, it was through her love and discipline that I gained a foundation that has allowed me to stay focused and persevere. I am also thankful to my children for their love and strength to help through the rough times and a special thanks to my writing partner Pearl Upchurch for staying up late at night to help me type out my writing. Finally, thank you to **You** for purchasing this book and supporting my dream.

Table of Contents

Traveling Mercy

I know that you are leaving
Know you will be missed
Before you go, grant me one final wish
Always stay healthy
Always be bless
Every goal you reach for may it end in success
And when life gets too crazy and you can't handle it all
Do me a favor
Please pick up the phone and give me a call
I Love You

Vision

To achieve life's goals
Although it will take hard work
Guts and ambition
You cannot, you will not, you shall not
Make it without prayer, faith and vision
Prayer, faith and vision
Go together hand and hand
It's like love and marriage
It's like woman for man
You have to believe in your dreams
And every day work toward it
Step by step
Day by day
Soon you will be rewarded
Visualize it, as if you already have it
Its right there in front of you, just reach up and grab it
Never, ever, ever
Forget to pray

Because Jesus is the light that will guide you on your
way
Now this part is important
Listen close to me
Don't give up
Don't accept negativity
Pray for it, believe it, seek it, receive it
It's yours.
Amen.

𝔓𝔯𝔬𝔭𝔥𝔢𝔱

Are you having problems?
Feeling sad and blue?
Then head on down to my church
I'll say a prayer for you
Ill anoint your head with oil
Tell you to have faith
But you know before you go you have to leave
something in my plate
Not tryna change your religion
Don't care how you believe
But don't you dare leave out of here without a donation
please
A twenty, a fifty, a hundred
OOOOhh that sounds real nice
But if you want the real long prayer
You gotta pay a higher price
I got a house with a great big mortgage
My Caddy needs new rims
I got two boys off in college who like to wear them tims
I gotta young wife who loves diamonds and a daughter
wrapped in mink

You might think I'm greedy
But I don't care what you think
You see this church thing is big business
Nothing of this world is free
And I'll make a way to get to you if you can't come to
me
Please keep in mind
Don't waste my time
I can arrive early or I can arrive late
But please know before I go, you gotta leave something
in my plate

𝔐𝔬𝔳𝔢

You are my daughter,
You're always be daddy's little girl,
You mean more to me than anything in this whole wide
world,
But now that you're older,
You don't want to hear anything I say,
You feel like you're a woman,
And you just refuse to obey,
You call me stupid,
And say my thinking is old fashion,
You even yell I hate you,
And you say it with such passion,
Well I've been doing some thinking,
And I want to make things right,
Because like I said I love you and it hurts me when we
fight,
Now here's my suggestion, and I really hope that you
approve,
If you're so unhappy,

Pack your stuff and move,
Start buying your books,
And paying your own tuition,
Then you can do as you please, you don't need my permission.
Hang out all night, feel what it's like to be free,
Just start buying toilet paper, toothpaste and paying electricity
Get your own apartment, say and do whatever you want,
Just make sure, make sure you have that man's rent on the first of the month.
Because if in this house is where you choose to stay,
Know that I'm in charge, and we do things my way,
So the solution is simple,
No need for you to be walking,
Around here shouting, pouting, with a nasty, stink attitude
The answer to your problem is simple, move.

Confused

Everyone around me is different,
There's Black, there's White, there's Spanish,
Tell me why we can't all just get along,
How come we can't all manage?
Was Martin Luther King a joke?
Encouraging unity and peace,
His dream was, racism must cease,
What about Travon Martin?
Was he shot for what he was?

God knows the answer because he looks down from
above,
Other countries want to kill us,
And blow us all apart,
Yet we won't work together,
As a people, that's really not that smart.

A Little Boy's Tears

You and your son came into my house,
Like you were a friend to me,
But it turn out, you were our enemy,
You were envious and jealous of what we had,
A brother, a sister, a mother, a dad,
You laugh and grin in my mom's face,
All the while planning to take her place,
So you shook your big butt,
Wore a tight blouse,
Made my weak father walk away from his vows,
And I cry for a while, every minute of every hour,
But it doesn't matter, cause in the end,
We all have to answer to a higher power

Afraid

You question me, about the other day, when the brother
jumped in my face.
You feel I should have knocked him out and put him in
his place.
You said I let him diss me, made me look afraid.
I should have pop a cap in him and sent him in his
grave.

Well my young friend,
Let me explain something to you.
Because part of what you say, happens to be true.
I am afraid of not being around, to watch my son become a man,
Afraid of not being near, to answer life questions he doesn't understand,
Afraid of not being close, to show my daughter love and affection,
All because one foolish moment of indiscretion
Maybe the brother had a lot on his mind, Maybe he was high,
Because the brother yelled at
Me, you feel that he should die?
Today I shoot him, tomorrow his brother shoots me, the next day my brother shoots his brother
Continued insanity?
You know life and freedom are so very precious,
I thank God for them both each and every day,
So if your question is, was I afraid?
The answer is yes, that's why I walked away.

New Birth

Congratulations on you brand new birth
A gifted child placed on this earth
Nine months of discomfort and some sacrifice
But it was all worth it to bring forth a life
I'm sure you will raise her with patience and love
Trusting in the man who sit up above
A teacher, a lawyer
A well known physician

Her grace, your strength will prepare her for any
position
You will stand back and watch as she takes on the
world
And think with great pride there goes my girl
Her elegance and beauty must always shine through
They have no choice because she takes after you
Let it be known
You are an inspiration once again
Congratulations!!!!

Daddy's Little Girl

Sometimes I'd wake up frightened in the middle of the
night
You rush into my room and always hold me tight
I remembered feeling love so secure wrapped in your
arms
I knew one thing for sure,
The Boogie man can do me no harm
And I know that you were tired at the end of the working
day
But you always took time to talk, to hear what I had to
say
You would listen to me patiently then gladly give your
advice
But you let me make my own decisions
And I always thought that was nice
You sacrificed so many times to provide the things I
thought I needed
Like pedicures, manicures and even hair weave
Been more than just my father, a lot
My real close friend

Stuck by me through it all, though, I've let you down
time and time again.
Like when you spent up all your savings and sent me off
to school
Instead of studying I partied and acted like a fool
And when I had my final separation form my lazy
abusive spouse
Your greeted me with open arms
Welcoming both me and my child into your house
Never showing your anger, never saying I told you so
Never putting a time on when we had to and because of
you guidance and assistance
And all your parental help
It enabled me to return to school to better life for myself
So I just want to say thank you for dealing with me and
my crazy mixed up world
I love you always and for you I give God praise
From Daddy's little girl

KKK

They use to wear long white sheets and cut up white
hoods
Say we were lazy, shiftless, and no good
Snatch us from our homes
Do as they please
Like kick us, whip us
Hang us from trees
These are some of the negative things
That the Klu Klux Klan did
But now, KKK stands for
Kids Killing Kids
My fourteen year old cousin

Got himself a nine
Out there acting fool, during lots of crime
Finally got caught now he's doing time
They tell him when to drink
They tell him when to eat
Lights out juvi
It time to go to sleep
No emotional growth
Mind not being stimulated
You gotta do what they say
When you're incarcerated
They told him to get on his knees
But he refuse obey
Let them know he doesn't go that way
Found him dead in the shower just the other day
Correction officer said it was done
By the KKK
Kids Killing Kids
A fifteen year old boy, said his thirteen year old
girlfriend showed him disrespect
So he took out his switchblade
Gave her seven stitches across the neck
Said he don't know why everybody so upset
It had to be done, to keep his woman in check
Her seventeen year old brother
Seen him shopping at the mall, the other day
Walk right up to his and took his life away
Respect given by the KKK
Kids Killing Kids
Calvin Evans, got himself an AK47
Sitting home all day getting high
At nine thirteen she does a drive by
Sitting on her porch is little three year old Maciah
It ain't his fought he got caught in the cross fire

Now her mother heart is filled with pain
No longer can they play the number alphabet game
No longer can they watch movies, very late at night
Or can she carry her to her bed and tuck in real tight
No longer can she look out the window
Just to watch her daughter play
Why Because of the KKK
Kids Killing Kids

Wake Up

Hey my people wake up please
Dying off from drugs and disease
Gang bangers up to no good
Selling off stuff in our neighborhood

Babies having babies collecting welfare
Just another form of control
DON'T ANYBODY CARE!!!

Brothers killing brothers over what they call a turf
Tell me was it all worth it

Unemployment going up, homelessness is becoming
bigger and bigger

After all we fought and marched for as a people now we
call each other nigger

Somebody tell me when will we be
Judge by the character within and
Not by the color of our skin

And those of you who are fortunate enough to make it
Don't move and up and try to fake it
Come back and pull somebody else out
After all, that's what real success is all about

Don't forget there's strength in unity
This is no time for us to break up
My brother, my sister
I LOVE YOU
PLEASE WAKE UP!!!!

Speak the Truth

When a woman falls in love with a man,
She will love him through thick and thin,
Not only is he her lover, but most times her best friend.
So if she ever leaves him, for whatever the reason might
be.
Don't be sad or upset, she just might be tired or have a
need to be free.
Now if she does return, their relationship could always
last,
But if she doesn't know for sure somebody else is
hitting that ass.

Told You

Explain this to me, because I'm somewhat confused,
If you think about it, it's a form of mental abuse,
Why is it?
When life beats you down,
And trouble boxes you in,

You need a little pick me up,
So you go talk to a friend,
Instead of making you feel better,
They hit you with a real low blow?
First they tell you,
"Hey! I told you so ! I told you so!"
What does that change?
Don't they know you already know?
You're the one to blame,
How about some words of encouragement?
How about some form of hope,
Why, Oh Why, Oh Why
Do they choose this time to gloat?
I told you, you shouldn't buy that house,
I knew you wouldn't get far,
Remember I said it was lemon before you got that car?
You knew she was unfaithful, I told you he would
cheat,
Both me and your doctors said lay off all of them
sweets,
So if you having problems,
Talk to the man up above,
He will help you solve them and He will show you love,
Cause if you have a friend who kicks you when you're
feeling low,
Maybe that's not really your friend,
Remember I told you so

(Thinking of You Wedding Vows)

Male - When I think of You, I think of a life lived
happily,
A bonded partnership for all eternity,
When I think of you.
Female - When I think of You, I think of our life
together,
Making it through good and bad weather,
Know because of you, life is much better
And this happiness will leave me never,
When I think of you.
Both - When I think of you, I think love,
Given to us from the man up above,
Because he's the one that we both serve and trust
His grace and His mercy smiles upon us.
Know that my heart will always be true,
This is what I think of, when I think of you.

Pity Party

Hurry! Hurry! Come one, come all,
Don't be scared, don't tardy,
I'm about to sit back,
And give myself a pity party,
Angry grim face, stink attitude,
Only music playing, sad, sad blues,
The food with be tasteless,
The drinks are all sour,
Pain and misery will be the host of the hour,
The first to appear was negativity,
Then frustration, arrive,
Sorrow appeared a little bite later with tears filling her
eyes.

If I should've, could've, would've came bringing his
entire crew,
I was so depressed; I didn't know what to do,
Just sitting around whining and complaining,
Hanging with all of my boys,
Till hope kick open my front door,
And said hey! Shut up all that noise.
He ran up to me and jumped in my case
Said
I can get you out of here if you only have faith!
Don't you know there are people out there worst off
than you?
The only difference is they don't just sit around all day
going boo hoo, boo hoo, boo hoo.
Now here's what you've got to do,
Look up, get up, and pull yourself together,
It might not happen overnight, but soon things get
better,
Well, it took a little while
Then I decided to heed hopes advice,
And I will admit, little by little, things are turning kind
of nice,
Know everyday isn't great
Nor have I reached perfection
But one thing for sure I know more live in the house of
depression

Money

As I write this poem,
I'm telling from the start,
Whether we admit it or not,
It about a subject that near and dear,

To most of our hearts
Now you might agree or disagree
Say I'm ignorant, gullible, or funny
But this poem is about one thing
Money
That tiny piece of paper, colored pea soup green
Can always, make life better,
No mater bad things seems
It can be the first thing on your mind in the morning
Or have you lying awake at night
It has been a subject of many arguments
Cuts and fights, money will make you do things you
said you would never do
It can make you smile or cause you to go boo hoo, boo
hoo
It will have male and female, dance around in their
birthday suit
It will have gorgeous women, tell ugly men hey! You
kind of cute
They say you can't buy religion, and it doesn't increase
your faith
Then how come, every time I'm in church they always
pass the plate
After the singing, clapping and long drawn out
confessions
My brothers and sisters prepare yourself for a collection
It's the reason why Mexicans landscape
Haters hate
Landlords love section 8
And winning the lottery feels so great
Now I've heard people say, they can live without it,
I don't know how they go about it,
True fully I doubt it,
Euro, Dinero, Mula, or Cheddar,

No matter what you call it you know it make life better.
If you drop it someone will grab it,
If you leave it out someone will steal or nab it,
Now I don't know about you, but I gotta have it,
Give me some Money.

Broken Hearted

I have a bit of a confession,
You see I'm going thought a depression,
Because I can't stop obsession over loosing you,
When I wake up I hurt, when I lay down I hurt.
It like my mind, soul and body was dragged through
some dirt.
Everybody I see remind me of you,
I want to be strong
But still all I do is boo hoo, boo hoo, boo hoo,
It was May 25th, no wait, May 26th the day it all
started,
That's when you pack your bags, wave good bye,
And left me broken hearted,
My friends tried to take me out, they all tried to make
me laugh,
They fell I should look to the future, and forget about
the past.
Everybody tells me this will someday end,
My only question for them, is somebody tell me when?
I never thought this could happen to me,
Who would think I could be out smarted,
I guest being very educated doesn't keep you,
For ending up,
Broken Hearted

You abuse me, misused me, made me feel like lest then
a human being,
You attack me verbally harass me, how could you be so
mean?
You deceived me, then you leave me/ please believe
me,
That was whack!
Still I love you, keep thinking of you, and want to hug
you,
Please come back,
Does that make me stupid? Foolish? Or just plain
retarded,
Maybe all three, cause if it's easy to see,
That the mind isn't free,
When you're Broken Hearted

Real Serenity

There's this little story, I like to tell,
About the day I promise myself, no longer to dwell,
On my past failures and negativity,
I took all the mistakes I made,
Rap them up, past them in the grave,
And label them history,
Them I use my mind and took my time,
To build a better me,
And with perspiration and dedication,
The outcome was victory,
You see, I've learned that life has its challenges
And it comes with certain rules,
But in the end the life we live is the life we choose

Should've, Could've, Would've

Shoulda coulda woulda, is a statement of regret,
It means you did or didn't do something that now has
you upset
It means that there's something that you need to change
Break it down, fix it up, so the outcomes not the same,
Don't you just wish that there was some way to reach
back to the past?
Think things over, slow it down, and not decide so fast,
Shoulda Coulda Woulda, is in love with yesterday,
Cause if you knew then, what you know now,
Your problems fade away,
Shoulda coulda woulda, fills you with
Anger, bitterness and hate,
Maybe next time you'll learn from your
Shoulda coulda woulda
Mistakes

Chance

Today I've decided to take a chance
Open up and try romance
I may have given myself real sparingly
But with patience and love
You have shown you care for me
So here's my heart gently take it
I've learned to love again
please don't break

Confessions

I'm smooth as silk, slippery then snot

You say I did it, I say I did not
You say I'm the blame
It's all my fought
I say no way
Cause I never got caught
You tell me speak up
Go ahead and confess, just admit, I'm the cause of this mess
Well my naïve friend, you don't understand, telling on me
Is never part of the plan, my goal is make you hear everything I say
Think things over, then see thing my way
I'll make a sad face, I might even cry, on some occasions
I've been known to lie, my model is
Deny, Deny, Deny
I ain't no snitch: I'm no body's flunky
I'm more like the deaf, dumb, blind monkey
So if you don't have proof that it was me, do me a favor, just let me be
Because everything I told you happens to be true, if you don't believe that
Go ask the blind man, cause saw it too

Me

I admire you, desire you and at time require
But at all times I need to be me
In this country we call America
Freedom is one of the greatest commodities
So why would you want to take that from us
When we said I do, it didn't mean I control you or you
control me
It meant I do believe that our life together would be
better
I do respect you thoughts and feelings
I do like having you in my life as I become complete
But know that I do still and always will have a need to
be me
Challenges and temptations come so easily in today's
society
I do have fantasies and dreams
Some I can share with you, some I can't (yet)
But know that you are my biggest fantasy and my
dream come true
So please just sit back, relax and let me be me

Party Hearty (Song/Rock)

Laying in a box an eternal bed
Eyes closed flowers surround your head
People stand around all dressed in black
Up drive the hearse Cadillac

They bowed their heads in prayer as the cold winds
blow

And then all said and done, you drop 6 feet below
People walk away with tears in their eyes
All of them tell those beautiful lies
Oh he was so nice
What a wonderful person

And then they party
They really party hard
Because life is to be lived so give all you can give
Because you never know you might not be here
tomorrow

Gotta Get Away (Song/R and B)

Now I know you've been out there foolin around
Running with some other girl in this town
And I'm not gonna get all mad and upset
No, no baby and go
And do something I think we'll both regret

But right now this very day I've just got
Gotta be on my way
Cause I know what I must do
I Gotta Get Up and Get Away from you, Girl!

Choir: gotta get away, gotta get away
Away from you, who, away from you
I just gotta get away, gotta get away, away from you,
who

We been through this to many times before
I'm fed up, I'm not gonna take anymore
Cause you promise me you were gonna change

But I find out that you still play that game
I gave you all the love a person can give
You became my life
My only reason to live
How could you do this when you know I've been true?
I'm gonna get up and stay away from you
You been out there cheating on me
Creeping on me
Now you think you gonna
Comeback and be sleeping with me
Don't you know there's a lot of deadly things out there
You could have killed us both and you didn't even care
I know exactly what your problems is you need to grow
up stop acting like a kid
Don't you know you're not seventeen anymore
Out there tryna see how many times that you can score
Now you come in here with some roses tonight
Thinking that's supposed to make everything right
But not
tonight boo
I through
I'm gonna get up and stay away from you

Father God Help Us All (Reggae Song)

Father God please help us all
I want to stand but all I do is fall
My pay is low and my bills are high
I'm on my knees each and every night
Asking you for better days
Because I know that Jesus saves

Then give me something from his account
Don't need a lot just a small amount
Nowhere to turn my back against the

Father God Please Help Us All

Went by my doctor on the other day
I didn't like what he had to say
The foods I eat are much to greasy
I'm overweight and I have diabetes
My pressure low and my cholesterol high
If I don't change my ways ill surely die
So I ask the Lord to help me through
Without his strength I could not do
Exercising day and night, counting calories and eating right
I'm feeling good and I'm standing tall
Father God He Helps Us All.

Woke up one morning feeling sad and lonely
Like I was the one and only man
Who could not find a wife?
Settle down and have a life
Now please don't go and get me wife
I had a lot of friends because my game is strong
But I was tired of different ones every night
I was looking for misses right
So I looked to my heavenly father
Said I don't mean to be a bother
But can you send me that special someone
I'll make her my wife and ask her to have my son
Now God is good and he always answers prayers
Cause I've been married for 7 lonely years
Family pictures hanging on each and every wall

Father God Helps Us All

Hard Head Makes a Soft Behind (Rap Song)

You started out young and rules you had none
The streets was you passion
You call momma old fashion, cause nobody mattered
but you
But as soon as you're in trouble you call momma on the
double
Cause she's the only one you can turn too
She said son I'll be right there
Cause to me you're very dear
But like I tell you time after time
You should do what momma say
Try your best to obey

Cause a hard head makes a soft behind

And you never listen to your dear old dad
But deep inside I know you wish you had
He told you to go to college
Hit the books and grab some knowledge
He said son don't be like me
Waste all your life in a factory
Go on to school and get that degree
You didn't listen, you never had the time

A Hard Head Makes a Soft Behind

So I heard you found you a brand new lady
Been messing around now she's having your baby
But everybody told you she wasn't ready
She out with a different man every night
You went and fell for that same old game
She's pregnant now and it's you to blame
It doesn't matter you really don't care
Cause you know she always count on welfare
But things didn't work out you thought
Look at your check
They do it to you every time
Play with your heart and steal your mind
Man don't you know that love is blind

A Hard Head Makes a Soft Behind

Now I see you've got a brand new love
You messing with that stuff they call drugs
I know somebody told they'll do you in
And you ought not go and mess with them
But you said un-un-no-no not the kid
Won't get hooked on them like other people did
I only use them when I'm feeling down
And blue and besides I can stop whenever I wasn't too
So you start out and you take a puff
Now a few years later you've using hard stuff
And you're walking the street with you mind in a haze
Thinking about when you had better days
When your money use to buy you real nice clothes
Instead of putting all that white stuff up your nose
Now you look a mess and you're all depressed
And you really do feel bad
I know you must confess
You didn't use them and your life was fine

You never once even thought about dying
It's too late to start crying
A Hard Head Makes a Soft Behind

Get Off My Back (Song/Comedy)

Friends I want to tell you a story about my wife.
The way she complains all the time and tries to run my
life
Used to be such a shy girl with nothing much to say
But every since I said I do
She talks 24 hour a day

Get off my back woman
Get off my back

I'm tired of fussin and fighting
And doing all of that
Well about ten years ago I said the word
I do
I don't mine the words
Just who I said them to
She makes me do the ironing
She even make me clean
You may think I'm a coward
But this here woman's mean
And you think that would be enough
Shucks that ain't even all
I don't even get to watch
My Monday night football
Get off my back women

Get off my back
I'm tired of fussing and fighting
And doing all of that
Now I'm getting tired of this
I'm gonna head for the door
Get off my back woman
Don't bother me no more
One day she gonna realize I'm the best thing she ever
had
But then it gonna be too late, cause her nagging gonna
have me dead
When you come to my funeral I don't want you to be
sad
Cause then I won't have to hear her mouth and boy will
I be glad

Get off my back women
Just get off my back
I'm tired of fussin and fighting
And doing all of that
So just say so long because I'm gone
And I won't shed no tears
All I need is my car keys
Good- bye ten wasted years

(Song) Ghetto Love

I know you're not so used to me being so forward
But the thing is, I really adore ya
Every since the day that I saw ya
I hoped that you'd be mine
I played hard, tried to hide the way I feel
Till you said boo, come on keep it real

Let's get together, get up out of these projects
Don't cheat on me and always give me respect
Now when we're apart, you're all I'm thinking of
I guess what I'm experiencing is this thing called ghetto
love.
(Chorus)
Ghetto love, Both going through the struggle
Ghetto love, tryna stay up out of trouble
Ghetto love
Working hard to make ends meet
Ghetto love
Who ever knew it could be so sweet?
You stood by my side that time I got locked up
When I came out that's when you got knocked up
I promised then, I would never go back
I gave up all the cars, jewelry and stacks
I'd rather spend time with my kids and wife
Thank God for a band new life
Showering me with his blessings from up above
Let me experience this thing called ghetto love
(Chorus)
Ghetto love, both going through the struggle
Ghetto love, tryna stay up out of trouble
Ghetto love
Working hard to make ends meet
Ghetto love
Who ever knew it could be so sweet?
Look at us girl we finally made it out
Living real large in this spanking new house
But we never forget where we came from
I like to go back and yell at the young ones
I let them all know how it once was
But I found strength because of ghetto love
(Chorus)

Ghetto love, both going through the struggle
Ghetto love, tryna stay up out of trouble
Ghetto love
Working hard to make ends meet
Ghetto love
Who ever knew it could be so sweet?

Thank You

Two little words that mean so much
Let it be known that I am touched
By all your love and tender kindness
It's very rare to find someone who really cares
You hardly ever find this
Often times, when we're in need
We'll make a request and we'll say please
But as soon as the task is through
We sometimes forget to show our respect properly
By saying thank you
Now to make this plain and simple
What I'm really trying to say is thank you, thank
you, thank you
In a very special way
I couldn't have done this without you
You played a very important part
Again thank you and God bless you
From the bottom of my heart
THANK YOU AND GOD BLESS YOU FROM THE
BOTTOM OF MY HEART.

9 780692 262283